So What? F**k It
A Guide to Internal Warfare

So What, F**k It!

DArren Murugan

Published by DArren Murugan, 2024.

While every precaution has been taken in the preparation of this book, the publisher assumes no responsibility for errors or omissions, or for damages resulting from the use of the information contained herein.

SO WHAT, F**K IT!

First edition. April 26, 2024.

ISBN: 979-8893795646

Written by DArren Murugan.

I would like to thank God for giving me life.

WRITTEN BY
DARREN YOGANADEN MURUGAN
Contents

This book is written for all those who long and yearn for freedom. If you are a prisoner of your mind you will always be subject to the turbulence of the external world around you. To the ones who ponder on the meaning and purpose of their lives, I love you.I do my best to give you a guide to your internal world and how to manage it. Coming from the culmination of my experiences and doing the shadow work to overcome certain challenges, these are the lessons I found helpful during my odyssey to peace. I sincerely hope you can draw something helpful from this guide. Thank you in advance for your attention.

1.Freedom

As obvious as it sounds in order to derive as much as you can from this limited life one must embody freedom. But that encroaches on the question as to what freedom truly is? Simply because one is not bound by chains does not mean that he is free, sure he is a free man but he may not be a liberated man. So, let's explore!

I should preface by saying in the culmination of all my experience thus far I have found there to be 5 freedoms in which if correctly ascertained one can reach absolutely and unequivocally the state of liberation.

I will immediately contradict my last statement using my first freedom, the freedom of the mind. One could say that liberation of the mind is all one needs as the mind is itself the perceiver in that if it perceives itself to be free then it is so, regardless of all the other freedoms. In fact, none of the other freedoms can be enjoyed unless this freedom is first obtained. This is why there are prisoners who can have more freedom than some of our billionaires. It is just that these intangible factors go unnoticed by many, as most of us see and judge only on the surface and instinctively overlook the feeling or concept of sonder, that should be in the forefront of our minds when assessing an individual or their lifestyle.

Firstly, to discern what it means to free your mind we must understand what the mind is. In my unlicensed opinion, I would separate it into two categories the first being ego and the other one being love. Now I appreciate that professionals would consider the superego to be the whole mind in which love and other feelings operate, but for the purposes of this book, I choose to categorize this as such.

Ego and love can be thought of as roots that are placed within the minds of every individual. One of the derivatives of ego is fear which can convert into anger, sadness, envy, self-pity and anxiety etc. And that of love is boundless and can derive into curiosity, creativity and fluidity etc. Fear will stifle the derivatives of love and will inevitably inhibit your performance. Anxiety and stress are unnecessary and will not improve or help in any way for the most part.

2. Separation

Sensitivity does not mean fragility or weakness. But just as we conflate ourselves with our mind, we conflate sensitivity to mean fragility. We look at it as a bad thing or a feminine trait. This is the issue with the human language it too readily conflates things and leaves meaning up to the egotistical mind. To enjoy the world and all that it has to offer you must be sensitive and not numb to it otherwise growth will be impossible. Think to be sensitive and also strong and resilient.

We often conflate ourselves with our minds. If we are not the mind then what are we. I think we are the observer the one that observes the mind. (Observer The Four Agreements). What does that mean? We host this body and mind. We are the driver not the car nor the engine. Some of us have a good car some beat up. Don't judge yourself by your car. Remember you are the driver.

In a rational evidenced-based explanation? There aren't any, at least not any I can think of to explain that we are the observers apart from the Four Agreements' point of view that we cannot have thoughts and observe them simultaneously.

Taking a spiritualist standpoint on the matter. We can say that the observer is the connector between the soul and our minds. Our intentions and feelings are simply conveyed through the observer and the mind becomes influenced by this intention. Remember we do not think through words but perhaps feelings and intentions.

They say that all the answers are inside of us. Perhaps that is what they mean. That our soul harbours infinite wisdom that has to be filtered to the mind. Now the question is how much of the soul can you capture through your mind? If you lack true belief in the soul's existence then you cut yourself off from the wisdom it can provide.

Some call that version of you your higher self.

When you decide to separate yourself from your mind you see the ego for what it is and easily catch it when it tries to lull you into insecurities. In this way, you realise that you are not your thoughts and that you are the owner of your mind. You will be more capable of controlling your emotions.

Sometimes with ADHD, the mind can take you the driver hostage through what we call maladaptive daydreams. You don't have to fight it. Go on this journey and analyse what it is showing you and why? ADHD is a blessing. It means you have great levels of sensitivity and an active mind. You have a stallion of a mind that sprints everywhere. The trick is that the stallion cannot stray too far from the rider. So get off the back of the horse and sit. Let the horse roam, it will have to come back to you. Remember you are not the stallion but rather you are the rider.

The observer? It is a skill. The spiritualists call it the third eye. The more you develop your third eye or observer the more you will be able to roam around your mind or inner world. The more you meditate and try to cultivate your observer self the more of an avatar you will create within yourself. You can now use this avatar to wander and explore the infinite worlds that lay within. I think that is what monks who have attained this skill or talent do with their hours of meditation. They roam around their minds exploring themselves.

Think about the saying that you eat when you are hungry, drink when you are thirsty, sleep when you are tired, and move your bowels when you need. I think that this is the instruction to simply maintain your body's basic rudimentary needs and the rest of the time spend it in meditation, wandering your mind and learning the lessons directly from it rather than learning the lessons indirectly from life. Or you could take it at face value to mean that you simply live free from stress and the worries of life.

3. The machine of the mind

Make the mind work for you. You hear it all the time but no one really explains how. We often find in my opinion very indirect and ineffective ways of going about taming it. Such as physical exercise that puts a strain and pushes one's will power to its limits. That is one way. But given the nuance and vast intricacies of the mind, we are only training one part of it that being willpower.

So begs the question, what are we doing when we train, tame, or control the mind?

Well as mentioned previously, one must not conflate himself with his mind. You are not your mind you are what observes it. Just as you are not the house, you are what dwells in it. You are not the car you drive it, nor are you the horse but rather its rider.

As mentioned above, seek to develop your observer self so that you may dwell and roam in your house with true and absolute freedom. Learn to face every room and corner of your house. This can be done with intention meditation trying to separate yourself at first. When you can differentiate between you and your mind, the roaming can begin. Remember to more you develop the observer, it will be like an avatar of your inner world. The avatar needn't look like anything, it can be whatever you want given that it is in your mind and thus your creation.

Just by realising this truth, you will begin to see and catch yourself falling into emotional traps. You will feel and notice your emotions. That is a step closer. Some of you may already be able to do this.

The Bhagavata Gita relayed that the mind can be your friend or your enemy. I always understood the enemy part. In that, you will fall victim

8

to the negative thoughts and doubts among other things that intrusively enter your mind. But the friend part, I simply thought of it as your mind no longer churning negative thoughts. But soon I realise when you separate the mind from yourself, you now see the mind as a machine just as one sees his body.

Thus the machine of the mind came about. Now, the mind is a very versatile, adaptive, and boundless living thing. It is scary just to think about it. It's like a wild animal, if raised terribly, will devour its host, but if raised in a nurturing environment will nurture and protect its host.

Making your mind your friend/ally/protector and perhaps subservient to you. If you want to be a comedian. Train your mind to look for jokes in everything. Look for jokes in everything you see. At first, you are going to have to put more effort and time into locating, identifying, and developing the confidence to tell someone your jokes. As time goes on you will not have to think about it consciously. The mind will automatically start looking for jokes. Now you can be picky and choose the jokes you think have potential. By making this selection and speaking it, the mind will adapt to improve the jokes to be more suited to the ones you have selected. More scientifically the pathway between the neurons will shorten and what took you minutes to think of will now take you seconds.

You have successfully used the machine that is your mind to help you in your endeavour to pursue comedy.

This is just a simple example. You can cultivate a more discerning and detached mind. You can practice paying attention to detain and practice exercising critical analysis and probative thinking, to develop a more discerning mind due to job or environmental requirements. Remember your mind is versatile and malleable it will churn out whatever you feed it. Teach it skills and it will look for ways to employ it automatically.

We often blame the way we think on our environment, but the environment simply was a training ground that allowed your mind to adopt certain skills and defects. Given its malleable nature, you can unlearn the defects and skills if they hinder you and adopt others. Sometimes learning a skill will prevent you from adopting another so unlearn it. It is well within your power.

Cultivate your training grounds appropriately as to what you want to see from your mind. You want stronger will power then run a lot to the point where your minds start to dread it. If you want a wittier mind, then start free-style rapping and go on debates. If you want a more analytical mind i.e. one that is more problem solving then try to solve maths equations or do puzzles etc. you get the point.

Remember once you train it to do a certain thing. It will do it automatically, especially if you reward it for its help i.e. give it a dopamine hit. In this way, your mind is like a loyal pet.

Keep possession of the ball. If your mind or attention is the ball, keep possession of the ball at all times. Do not let others have possession of it freely or at all. You must guard it or rather train it to guard itself. Letting your mind fall victim to the perception and points of view of others ensures that you lose control of it. The mind must be impervious and elusive to the grasp of anyone else. This ensures that you maintain your freedom and that you cannot be manipulated by anyone. By placing too much value on the thoughts and opinions of other people you are telling your mind that they are in control and not you. It now serves and worships public approval/validation as it receives the reward (dopamine hit) every time. Meaning you are simply reaffirming that you are not in control.

This in addition to the conflation of you with your mind makes the mind such a messy, chaotic, and volatile place for you to live.

Unlicensed thought here but if you could observe the mind, wouldn't it be easier to understand and work through issues such as depression and addiction? You are not broken; you simply have to retrain your pet. It is pissing everywhere, barking at you, shitting on the floor, chewing on the couch, attacking the postman. That's okay. Just train it.

You can do it alone or get a good therapist to probe you in the right places. Make sure to work with them for if you resist it will not be as effective as it could and you end up putting a hindrance on the healing process.

"The jack of all trades is a master of none but still better than the master of one". Why is he better than the master of one? You see the master of one has gone so far down his chosen discipline that he cannot use or cultivate a competent understanding of other aspects of his mind as he has lost malleability. If you grow something, then something else has to give or gets sacrificed. The law of the universe. What I mean is that if you become the best problem solver you may compromise or sacrifice growth in emotional and social intelligence because you have cultivated and developed the mind to grow in a certain way for far too long. The good thing is that, if you take a break from the activities that engage that part of the brain then it becomes "rusty" allowing you to develop other skill sets. I am not saying that this is always the case but sometimes the parts that you don't know exist yet will be cut off and you end up limiting yourself.

At the very beginning, learn to grow in all aspects without going too far in a particular one. As time progresses and you reach a certain level at the desired traits then go on to master one. Your ability to unlearn something will come in handy. So, remember that sometimes you will have to undergo the process of unlearning and relearning a particular skill.

If you carelessly allow yourself to specialise in something particular at a young age particularly if you receive recognition for it, your personality may develop around this thing and so you adopt an identity around this specialty. Dangerous, if what you do is no longer seen as worthy of recognition you end up having an identity crisis.

The chaotic mind if it wanders then give it free rein use it to your advantage just direct it to a vague topic and let it rebound off the wall of just that topic. ADHD is a gift if you know how to use it.

ADHD for me is like a very bouncy ball that constantly picks up momentum relentlessly with every thought, especially on caffeine. So, use it like this. Take the bouncy ball and throw it into a room (room being a topic you like or a problem you have) and close the door. Now watch the ball (your mind) rebound off of every wall, surface, and corner looking at every angle. You see you do not have to stress out trying to focus on a singular point but rather just a large confined space will do the job. You will find it easier that way. Example how do I get a job? Let it work now. Put some effort and do not let it deviate or leave that room until you are done with that task.

Imagine having a mind that requires you to push like you are treading through mud. Not great, right? Thank God for your blessing of the hyperactive mind. Just because it is seen as a disability does not make it so, sure there are drawbacks but the positives outweigh them in my opinion. Everything has drawbacks. Depending on the severity of it, your experiences may differ as a result. But all in all, just find the positives and sit with those for a while before learning to tackle the cons.

Another example I like to give is the horse and the stable. The horse being the mind will gallop anywhere and everywhere. That is not a bad thing, you just need to be able to call the horse back to the stable. At first, it will be hard but as you try it will get far easier to do so. Unlike the horse that has to travel miles to get back the mind can get back to you in an instant. A more difficult problem is the horse that does not or refuses to leave its stables.

Sometimes, just like a terrorist the mind will take you hostage in maladaptive daydreams and you end up wasting a lot of time in what appears to be procrastination. When this happens especially if they happen often, start to write them down and analyse the common themes of these daydreams. We do not daydream for no reason. We do so because it makes us feel something whether it is good or bad and we have scenarios that we play into. This is the beginning of your shadow work. I believe the subconscious mind is trying to tell or teach us something about ourselves with maladaptive daydreams. When you break them down you may find answers or reasons why you behave or feel a certain way. For example, you can find out the root cause of your desires and fears and it can run as a common theme in the mind. If it gets too hard, talk them over with a therapist.

4. Comforts of life

There are powers or skills in life that if one can grasp may help you achieve and access more powerful versions of yourself. These are;

The Power to enjoy your own company: being complete and whole on your own.

Embracing and Accepting Death

Embodying the Law of detachment

The Power of shifting perception and beliefs

The power to shift your perception is closely tied to the power of belief. Belief has no end to it. Think about the placebo effect, the whole concept is tricking people into believing something that is not true but their body may react from a physiological standpoint as though the point in question were true.

This power will allow you to change the way you view yourself. You will not need anyone and you can find peace a joy in your own company among many other things.

How? The idea is not to love yourself because of a trait, a characteristic or how you are perceived by others but rather to accept yourself as you are. This will allow your love for yourself to be unconditional. Unconditional love means without reason. If you love something for a reason then that reason can be lost and so that love is conditional.

It can be more complicated than just expressed. To embrace and accept oneself as whole and complete may require you to shift your perception of how you view everything else. Perception shifts will change your perspective as to how you approach something if not everything.

A Perception shift may require a lot of work in that you may have to be self-critical and self-analytical before you can finally work through the realm of this new shift.

Think about it like this as kids we thought the world was nice, warm, and fluffy until we first came across a negative experience to give us a more balanced view. Say for example the death of a loved one, as children we would be unable to comprehend what has happened but now our perception has shifted as we are aware that our time is limited. How we approach life has changed in most cases drastically. we may begin to feel fear of the unknown to be expected from death. We may even become religious for answers and so on.

When a man shifts his perception, he may become a totally different human being entirely. You see by shifting his perception the web of thoughts that makes up his reality will also shift, in that way his projection and understanding of the world will forever change. That is what you gain through life experience (seeing the world differently). With the right shift, you will carry yourself differently. Your facial expressions will change as the muscles you are contracting and relaxing subconsciously will adjust accordingly. People will sense this from you and you will give off a different impression entirely. This is why some say to cut connections from the past as people knew you to be a different person and may prevent you from changing or fully embracing a new perception. You do not want to be stuck in a perception particularly if it is an unfavourable one.

So, shifting your perception will help you to accept and embrace yourself if you do not already do.

Most people may not understand this and believe that it is a simple tweak of one thought. But just simply because you think it, does not mean that you believe it. The shift of perception will be important in order to believe something. A thought or a belief is tied to another and another in a web of thoughts and beliefs. Sometimes finding the first thread in a web can be extremely difficult, so a perception shift is needed to change the dynamic of one's belief system.

The stronger the web of thoughts that confirm your current belief system the harder it will be to shift your perception into believing something new. For example, will you be able to believe that the sky is any other colour than blue say purple? It will be very hard as the thoughts that surround the belief that the sky is blue are so strong in confirming and reconfirming this fact that it will be very difficult to believe anything else. However, if you shift your perception as to what the color blue is and change it to mean purple instead then that belief can occupy reason in your mind. In that way, you can use the power of belief to your advantage.

A new perception can be adopted easily by those with an open mind. Open-mindedness when voluntary is a powerful tool but if unchecked can lead to naive actions or believing in falsehoods. But overall, when adopted correctly an individual with an open mind can pick and choose different perceptions to best suit him.

Which is why I think affirmations are not very effective. I could be wrong but if you can understand the root cause of why you feel a certain way you can start to shift your perception and start to believe in the thought you want to embody.

In my opinion, a perception shift is key to changing one's belief system.

So, shift your perception and start to embrace yourself.

Embracing and Accepting Death

E mbracing and accepting death as part of life and not something separate will help you put everything into perspective. Your constant remembrance of death or memento mori will help you let go of the things that will leave you void and focus on life in a more playful and non-serious fashion.

Embracing death will also help you to further tackle and release attachment to your ego. In particular, the value you place on the opinions of other people and their perception of you. As you will realise that their perception will die with them and yours will die with you. You will start to value what you think of yourself more than what others think of you. The release of this shackle will allow you to take a new lease on life. It will make you bolder, and less hesitant and you will not doubt yourself as much.

By accepting death, you will become a more powerful and carefree version of yourself. Believing in an afterlife will also help calm you but there is power to be had in the whole-hearted embracing of the ultimate unknown.

Embodying the Law of detachment

Detachment does not mean not caring but rather not allowing the actions of others to influence your internal world. To detach from materialistic things does not mean that you should not own anything but rather it prevents anything materialistic from owning you. For example, if you worship money, then money will own you. If you worship sex then sex will own you, if you worship public validation then the public will own you. Meaning they will own space in your mind and influence your emotions.

You do not want to be owned so detach your peace from these temporary things.

Understand that your time on this earth is temporary and so are the materialistic allures of this world. Your internal world is the only thing you have control over so do not allow anything to have any power over it.

You are in a story. The story of you. Most say you should be the Main Character of your story but I think that this is partly true. I believe that you should also try to be the audience member of your story not just the MC. You see the audience member also means to be the observer of yourself, to be able to take a step back and look at the scene with a somewhat objective lens.

By doing this you will be able to detach from the story itself understanding that this life in essence is almost like a play or a dream being acted out. Do not take life so seriously.

What does it mean to be attached? Attachment simply means to attach your emotions to something. It goes even further than that you see everything begins and ends in the mind. But by attaching your emotions to other people we allow them to be triggers for us. We inadvertently put levers and buttons on them that connect to our egos which they can use voluntarily or involuntarily to trigger our emotions. At this point, we are doomed because we are at their mercy. If you attach your self-worth to the opinions of your friends, then if they decide to pull on that lever and act in a way that is demeaning to you your whole self-worth will be compromised. The idea is that you should be mindful and cautious as to who bears your emotional triggers i.e. buttons and levers. You should strive to be emotionally connected but not emotionally attached in that way the self-destructive behaviour of others does not trigger you. You simply allow people to be themselves and you can love them anyway. Loving someone through connection rather than attachment allows you to be more pure, genuine, and selfless with your love. You will not be spiteful or vindictive if your love is not reciprocated in the way you want.

It is the ego that attaches to things. Try to play with the emotions that dwell outside the scope of the ego. That being among other things, righteous anger, unconditional love and contentment, etc.

This is easier done when you are a trigger for yourself. When you are able to tap into the unconditional love you have within you and direct it at yourself you will feel whole. The reason is that you do not need anyone else to love you for you to feel loved or feel worthy of being loved.

To know where your emotions are coming from just ask yourself why you feel the way you do and be honest with yourself. Are your emotions coming from a place of selfishness or selflessness?

An issue I always pondered on was desire. Say we did not desire, then sure we would be free. But sometimes it is fun to desire and it serves as a good driver. The issue is that with desire comes fear. How can we separate the fear? Is it possible? YES! Detach from the potential outcomes that you want. Simply trust the process and let the process guide you in whatever way it chooses to. Keep the goal in mind without letting yourself get attached to it. For example, if I want a six-pack, I will do the things I know are required to get it but I will not be attached to the outcome being how people will perceive my six-pack, the quality/ muscle insertions of my six-pack, and whether you get there, simply lose yourself in the process. Just do the work! You have now separated the fear and overthinking that can be associated with desire.

You can now attack or approach a project or a goal simply with desire as a tool rather than an anxious attachment.

The main goal ultimately should be to remove desire as a whole in doing this you will find true peace.

Summary

We often have quite a lot to uncover before we can be free or liberated in the mind. Usually, we go straight into it with no idea of how to begin. First, we must develop and cultivate the tools to dig up the dirt and cut down the roots. Developing and trying to understand the law of detachment, the ability to shift perceptions, embracing death, and predominantly the ability to let go or surrender among other things you might think of will serve as the shovel, spade, and axe to destroy the root. You see the root may be fear or a mixture of various negative emotions developed through trauma. To dig it up will mean that you will feel these emotions again. Not many want to do this. They would rather leave the root buried or even cover it up with even more dirt being the substance abuse or other distractions that we use to cope. In doing this you will give the root time to develop and even spawn new offspring. You may develop fear attached to this one root. Before you know it, you have a jungle of fear and negative emotional trauma in your mind guiding your everyday actions.

Remember, the root requires your energy for it to stay alive. This comes in the form of attention and that you give it. You see your emotions can only attach to the things that you give attention and time to. So to starve the root while it is still developing, look to separate the thought from the emotion. Take back your emotional energy and convert it into another emotion using your thoughts as the compass and guide. I will explain this form of control using your thoughts in detail another time.

SO WHAT, F**K IT!

For roots that have borne fruit, I would suggest the first method of taking time to develop the tools and hacking away. The truly talented among us only require the ability to let go. With this, they can release all trauma and pain in one go not needing the spade or the axe, etc. Don't despair if you are not one of these individuals, just focus on building your equipment for the time being. You may need a therapist if you cannot locate the trauma to help trigger you. Sometimes being triggered is a good thing, it tells you where your trauma is located and what fears you have. Upon identifying them you can let them go.

5. Start to accept yourself. Acceptance through faith or acceptance through defeat

The soul Finds it difficult to leave the body/ move on because it becomes too attached to it as a means of identifying itself. That's why the Hindus burn the body as it makes it easier to move on. The soul is trying to find itself/ understand what it is. In life, we identify as our name/profession/ talents/ looks/ relationships, etc and when those are stripped away, we do not know what we are any longer. So this confusion makes us lost and anxious which ''then perpetuates further fear and anxiety. This is the dilemma of the soul as these identities are forcibly stripped away upon death. The key is while living you must not wholly identify yourself with any of these. Soon the soul will find that it simply exists with no identity. "All I know is that I exist and I accept that". Once acceptance has been undergone then it can finally move on.

Perhaps growth can only occur in life through the body and maybe it is extremely hard for the soul in its rawest form to grow without this medium and the vast stimuli of the world. So in the world, we forget all the important things that we must do as we are being drawn in by every little distraction predominantly due to the ego's needs. When we leave the body without addressing our insecurities, fears, and lower emotions we end up bringing it with us to the other side as baggage or karma. How do we get out of this cycle, well it's simple the only thing you need to do is "let go". Let go of your fears, anger, insecurities, pain, trauma, shame and guilt etc. Letting go of everything outside of your control etc. Letting go is not just a statement it is a feeling. Once you can embrace this feeling you will inevitably free yourself from all of that baggage. It can be difficult. So practice. Eventually, you will train your mind to let go and it will. The soul has no mind and so how will it let go? So while we have the luxury of our bodies and minds we should utilise it in our endeavour to let go. This body of ours is a tool to help us unburden our souls of any past events and lower emotions be it in this life or the previous and thereby ascend. The Buddhists think of spirituality as not acquiring something but rather stripping away things from yourself and exposing yourself in its truest form. Children do this well as they lack the egotistical nature of their adolescent counterparts.

This concept can be difficult to understand as if you are letting go i.e of control then to whom? To Whom that is are you surrendering control, is it to God? The universe? Life? All of the above. Truth, is it doesn't matter what you can't control will never be in your grasp so stressing about it and focusing your attention on what is outside your jurisdiction will only cause pain and everything you want to avoid. Nevertheless, it can still prove quite the task, as previously explained letting go is not simply a statement to understand it is a state of being that can be reached or a feeling that can be acquired. An example is the perception of others, which are and always will be outside the scope of our control albeit, we may be able to influence it. That being said we should not act to influence the perception of man but rather this should be an indirect effect of the works and projects that we seek to undertake.

If one is religious then letting go to God is the best course of action. If one does not subscribe to any religion and is an atheist then it may be harder but still doable. Just think of the things that you can control these are; intentions, thoughts, words, actions, and emotions. When all of these are combined, we now have the ability to TRY. This ability is all we have in our control we can try to go to the gym but whether we arrive is not in our control. Outside of our ability to try is the realm where all things outside the scope of our authority reside.

Pondering about these things does nothing but cause anxiety, fear, pain, worry, stress, etc. So let it go!

Once you can truly do this regardless of religious beliefs or doctrines you will achieve a level of being known as "God's peace". This peace will let you live life in a liberated and freeing manner. You will find that the food that you eat will taste far better, even tap water can be enjoyed with this peace of mind. Just free yourself by relinquishing control. In that way, one can truly be in control. Nothing can harm you now as you are carefree. Do not conflate this with being careless.

Perception is all in the mind and is derived from the culmination of data provided by the sensory organs. However, the sensory organs are limited to their designed function. Meaning the perception of man is founded simply on the culmination of his own experiences, his bias, and the limitations of his senses. Very few are truly objective, very few will say I do not have enough knowledge on the matter to choose a side so I am coming into this with an open mind. Most care too much about how they will be perceived.

The table theory coined in this book was perhaps thought of before but is unknown to this author. Say there is a table in front of you and you cannot perceive this table through sight, sound, touch, taste, or smell. How would you know it was there? You wouldn't. it might as well not be here. We are our perception. Perhaps there are other senses that would allow us to locate or sense this table or perhaps the senses we have do not reach the frequency or aren't tuned enough to acknowledge the existence of this table. So, the table can be thought of as both existing and not existing simultaneously. It goes to show the power of perception to influence the individual.

Looking further into the table theory we can think about what other objects or entities are possibly existing and occupying the same space but outside of the scope of our limited perception.

In fact, should someone see the table through a different means we would more likely than not call them crazy given our influences in pop culture, our ignorance on the matter and lack of open-mindedness.

Taking this further beyond the table theory most spiritual doctrines believe that time is not linear but rather state that it is always stagnant but that we move through time. That we are only living in an ever-lasting now/present moment and that the future and the past are illusions and not in any realm of reality. So one theory that this author plays with is that everything that has ever happened or will ever happen is occurring right now at present but outside the scope of our perception. We do not have the faculties to perceive or access the perception of these events transpiring. This I call the forever now theory.

6. Peace in the Now

We fight to be happy, we fight to feel joy, we burden ourselves with an overwhelming effort to chase these feelings of pleasure. But one must denote that these too can be considered as lower emotions. Just as sadness, hate, and jealousy are lower emotions their positive counterparts can be labeled as such too.

Don't chase these feelings, if they come let them and be open to the experience of allowing them to flow through you. Just because you feel a negative lower emotion does not mean you are of bad character. Do your best to catch yourself feeling these and try to observe them and comprehend what triggered them to come forth. When you are able to do this you will be able to observe them in others, you will gain a power of discernment, and see and notice those who are subscribing to their lower emotions.

The key is to look for peace. Sounds very obvious but peace is the most stable, consistent, and reliable state of being one can attain. Peace is a state of being not an emotion or maybe we can think of it as being both. Peace can be attained through the acceptance of life and death. You feel acceptance even when you are sad or happy.

The bubble of perception. The concept of sonder is that each person has as complex lives as our own. We each have our own story to work through, we just get so caught up in our own story that we forget other people are living out their own. One way of thinking about it would be to look at any person and realize that they were all babies at one point even the oldest man or woman were cute babies.

All we are, are just stories. If our perception of who we are is based on what others think we are, this will mean that they are in control of our stories. We communicate and interact with each other through the bubble of our perception.

You may occupy the same physical space as someone but be in completely different worlds to them that is because the bubbles of your perception is not overlapping but bouncing off of each other and preventing you from reaching them. Our bubbles may overlap like that of a parent and child, but they do not occupy the same bubble no matter how close they are. The way to deal with this is to expand your bubble and perspectives keeping an open mind and reforming the ways in which you form a perception. Some would say that this approach would move to eradicate the bubble entirely and allow you to move seamlessly through other people's perceptions.

The bubble of perception can be best thought of as a bubble of your story. For example, it is not until something or someone enters your bubble that you start to perceive it and incorporate it into the story of your life. Example: you are walking through the woods and you stumble upon a river. By coming across the river, you now incorporate it into your storyline, say you are thirsty you now perceive the river as a good thing, a source of water. Say you need to cross the river but the current is very strong, now the river is perceived as a bad thing. Not until it enters the bubble of your perception will you even think about the river. Human beings are the same.

Something cannot be good or bad without you being there to perceive it as such. By eradicating your bubble of perception and just taking things as they come not as good or bad but just as it is, then you can find the peace in any situation and overcome it mentally. When you cannot enter the bubble of another person it means that you cannot be incorporated into their story and vice versa. But with no bubble, you can go anywhere you want freely. (Repetitive I KNOW)

7. The honest con man: we are selling for the price of an ego pump

Everyone and their mother are salesmen. Some of us just don't know it. We are selling ourselves all the time be it for a job, for friendship, community etc. you change the way you behave, dress, and speak in an attempt to better sell yourself. Seldom are we selling our true selves it is always a self that we pretend to be that we call our best selves. Is it our best self if it isn't even us but rather a self that we develop in our attempt to fit in? why do we call the self that we use to fit into societal norms and culture our best self? I guess it's primal in that it once helped as a tool for survival. But now it only serves to mask your authenticity and individuality. You end up becoming a mimic of society. If the world and people are a reflection of your inner mind then you the one trying to fit in becomes a reflection of what you think your reflection is, which means that you become the reflection and not the original. Imagine standing in front of the mirror and trying to copy your reflection that is what your best self is by today's standards. Now, balance, conform where needed but do not lose sense of self or individuality.

The actual salesman. In society, those who sell as a profession understand the game of selling. Understand the untold, unspoken truth that everyone is selling something to someone or even to themselves. The salesmen dress, speak, and behave with the intention of selling. He hones his craft whether going by a script at first or building and developing on his shortcomings with the sole purpose of selling. You the salesman know about the gift or trait of likability. He understands that it is not the product or service but rather how he comes across to the mark. He

understands the psychology involved and how to persuade with his gifts. You see in my opinion it isn't just hard work that sells but rather likability in the form of charm, looks, etc. Think about it he can make himself appear in such a way that the mark seeks his approval. It is a game of appearance and seldom substance. Most of us go simply from our ego and vanity.

Usually, female salespeople are very bubbly, fun, carefree, and pretty. They make you feel encapsulated by the energy. It helps them to sell particularly to men. Vice versa the handsome, groomed, charming, and well-spoken men sell to both men and women. The men want to be involved and included as part of the group and usually cooperate with the sale.

This is not a sales book. The purpose of this is to explain how those who know that they are selling have the advantage of intention. They cater themselves to what they know their mark will fall for. They understand that not everyone will be their mark so they lend themselves to a particular demographic rather than allocating their time and effort equally to everyone.

The rest of us who do not know are throwing darts at a board in a dark room. We just hope we hit a mark.

If you desire to play the game which I try to avoid then at the very least adopt intention so you can play it effectively. Intention will also help you to separate yourself from the salesmen and thus be able to notice and identify your true authentic self.

8. Likability

As mentioned above likability is a powerful trait to have. It will give you such a boost in life. Some people are likable by nature, growing up in households with a lot of examples of likable people, they were set in a training ground that cultivated, taught, nurtured and rewarded this trait. Some need help to understand themselves more and their unique likable traits.

The best way to go about finding your likable trait is to ask what you find likable in others. What traits do you find attractive in others that you can adopt? Do not get lost in what you think others find likable. That is a sure way to get lost and unless your opinions coincide with others you will end up not liking your likable traits.

You cannot control some likable traits like looks, appeal, ethnicity, etc. If you have advantages here consider yourself lucky.

Likability means you can get away with things others may find it hard to. An example is stand-up comedy, where a controversial joke told by a comic with tremendous likability will be taken light-heartedly. He will get away with the offensive aspect of the joke. Likewise in society, the social offenses of the likable man will be overlooked in that he will not be held accountable for his actions or words as opposed to an unlikable individual. This is within reason; in that he cannot get away with egregious offenses. But society may likely overlook his trespasses.

This goes further, into the criminal justice system. You are tried by a jury of your peers. This will not result in true justice all the time. Think about it a jury will have biases that culminate from their life experience which may be relayed through their subconscious. At this time a man who does not bear likable traits will most likely be seen as guilty by the jury notwithstanding the evidence. A pretty young lady will likely be seen as innocent than a male inverse counterpart. Simply how we society judge each other will have its effects in the courtroom. We do have safeguards around this being the case going to trial if it fulfils the evidential burden etc, which is at the discretion of the judge. All in all, if you want to play this game then be aware that most of it is not in your control.

Do not get bogged down with other people's opinions of what likable is. A man's perception will die with him and yours with you. So be likable to yourself and if others agree, cool, if not Fuck it. I like me, so what if you don't?

Changing our creative ideas to fit the perception of man in placing too much value on how he will receive it puts a hindrance on the creative process. What we like to do may lead to other finer creative ideas that we cannot fathom at the beginning. But changing it to fit into the perception of society will take away from that. So, make your art without any care for its reception for the minds of men will forever be outside your control.

A Hindu concept is that one's life is determined by the karma of his previous life or his past misdoings or good deeds. One may say that Karma is not the event itself but rather our reaction to the event. For example, for a truly sensitive individual event x may have a devastating effect on his psyche but to the less sensitive individual, it may roll off his shoulder quite easily. What does that mean, it means that the two having experienced the same event perceived it at different levels of misfortune. what if we not only controlled our reaction but also our perception of the event? To best control your reaction you must change the way you perceive something. Changing your perception requires you to observe yourself and ask why you think the way you do. Perhaps it is the collective consciousness that causes you to do so as a way of fitting in and being accepted by the community to best further your survival.

But by not eliciting an emotional reaction to an event or by choosing not to perceive something as a bad thing you take away its power and it cannot hurt you. One way would be to look at why you saw an event in the past as bad and look at its roots. In that way, you can break down your perceptions of the story that is your life. You should look at your story or life as the audience member and not solely the Main Character in that way you get a better view and a broader and more objective understanding of what is going on. How do you control your perception? It is the man that makes heaven. Heaven is not a place but an experience. A righteous man can experience heaven in a hellish environment and a corrupt man can experience hell in even the highest of heavens. Heaven is a state of being as is hell that anyone can have access to.

Sometimes we desire or long for things. Longing for something is a normal part of life. It is said, that if we desire something then it is our higher self telling us that it is possible for us to ascertain ..... We learn about ourselves through our desires. However, desire has two ends these are what we want and what we do not want. What we do not want is the fear. Desire will inevitably come with fear. We must think about what we want to happen and not what we would not like to happen. In other words, one should think with love and not fear. Within the realms of reason whatever that means to you, you should not feel shame or guilt from a desire, instead, look at it and try to understand it. By attaching shame or guilt to it you may delay it. Sit back and seek to understand it. Let go of these feelings and appreciate your desire for what it is.

The yin of scarcity. The lack of abundance in something that you truly long for will provide you time to ponder and develop an appreciation of what it is you truly want. If you reach a level of appreciation for something that you long for but do not have, it gives you a very different relationship to desire. Now your desire is a point of love and not fear and its derivatives i.e. envy, anger, frustration, etc. For example, if what you desire is love try to appreciate love in all its forms and wherever you see it try to feel a sense of adoration or admiration for it whether or not it is targeted at you. In that way, you negate the negative lower emotions that may arise as a result of scarcity and it is this author's opinion that you will end up attracting more love into your life.

The head and the heart are so hard to control. Both must be used in a balanced sense. The term heart is used in its figurative sense. Where the mind can see no hope and wants to give up it is the heart that yearns and begs it not to, it is like the heart can see or feel something that the mind cannot. How many times have I tried to give up or lose hope or accept defeat but the heart just would let me believe it. The heart stops you from believing the doubts the negative self-talk or the feelings of sadness. The heart dreams, and desires and give you endless possibilities. But the mind will always look analytically with its senses. The bible says that when a man uses his emotion and thoughts as one he can move mountains. Maybe what was meant is that if you desire from the bottom of your heart with true emotion and you use your mind to find a way to attain it you will find what it is that you seek. So you need to balance every action between heart and head.

The time dictates the crimes. In that way what was seen as acceptable and ethical in the distant past could be considered atrocities in the present. In the same way, one should look at their perception. We try so hard to fit in that we mold ourselves into this creation that could be accepted loved and admired. But at what cost? We lose authenticity. We lose our true selves and what we were capable of reaching. Now we would have to strip away what we have become, strip away the ego, fear and allow ourselves to grow into what we should have been at first. This is truly hard, particularly for famous young people. They become so enveloped in ego and lose themselves in a world of public perception. They then know nothing else. They live and die on this hill and obtain very little growth at least from my perspective. Who's to say perhaps I am wrong? So if perception is determined by the times we are in and by the community, then lest we Mold ourselves for survival's sake we are outright conning ourselves into what we could have truly become, one that is the closest to our soul or nature's true expression of self.

You have to strip away all the fear, ego, the "I care about what people think of me" and insecurities and ask yourself "Who am I?" that's when your soul or your nature can truly express itself. One must cultivate different mediums of self-expression I.e. language, song, instrument, dance, and other forms of expression best suited to you. In this way, you are able to be the most authentic version of yourself and not just a copycat or a Mold of what you think is to be generally accepted. Think of the oceans of endless soul that resides within you. What faculties do you possess to express it or embody it? Do you have a cup or your hands or giant tanks to showcase the infinite body of water that is your soul to the world? "Best to live out your life imperfectly than to live the life of another to perfection". (Bagavad Gita)

There are many replicas out there those that are great but legends put their spirit into what they do as they have unravelled themselves from the cloak of fear and ego. When the curiosity to explore your fears is greater than the urge to run away from them that is when one develops a greater sense of being.

From a young age I wanted to be a doctor. It was predominantly superficial. My heart nor my soul was in it. I simply wanted it for its prestigious title. Given how half-heartedly I ended up in biomed, the not-so-recognized sibling of medicine. Then I did law and finance for the same reason however it did give me a better understanding of the world and a broader sense of practical knowledge in regard to these subjects. I mean name a country or society that does not incorporate finance or law into its system. I soon realised that a career in either field would leave in a void.

Albeit I am sure that my family and people around me would be impressed but who cares. I only have one life, why should I spend an inordinate amount of time and effort into something that would be solely for public marvel?

9. All is within me

You are a walking perception. The world is at the mercy of your perception or rather you are at the mercy of your perception.

Everything is happening in our minds. I mean everything. Think about it. Without the mind to perceive something it might as well not exist. Think about the tangible. Everything around us has to be processed by our brain and recreated into what it is. The eyes capture the information and the brain processes it to create the images we see. So in theory someone else could perceive the object through sight differently than another if their brain processed the information differently. Now think about the complexities involved in our perception of another human being given how complex we are.

Your perception of the person is not the person itself it is simply your idea of the person tainted with the bias and experience that you have learned through life, societal norms, and standards. An individual and their expression of themselves are two completely different things. As mentioned above. So how do we negate this, as human beings? We often look at the vain aspects of a person i.e. their appearance, socioeconomic status, dress sense, accent, looks, etc. We then make a general assessment. This judgment would be the same or similar to that of members of our community in that way we can assign a value to this person that others would agree with.

When the heart and the mind agree with each other no task is impossible. A spiritualist would say that this agreement is the frequency at which the soul or your entire being vibrates. The mind looks to believe and analyze predominantly through historical data (i.e. your past experiences). It will utilize and apply this to a particular situation that you are currently facing or likely to face in the foreseeable future. By doing this it will cause you to feel a certain emotion that if your heart agrees will bring about a state of being that your physical body emanates.

An example your mind may feel fear or cause you to feel fear, if your heart agrees with this emotion then you will experience a more tangible manifestation such as; panic attacks, nervousness and butterflies in your gut, etc. The intensity of the feeling will vary depending on how much the heart agrees. If only a little then butterflies, if a lot then panic attacks or far worse. Similarly, if your mind extrapolates the feeling of sadness with the agreement of the heart then the body will feel fatigued or discouraged, and it is with that vibration that you seek to pursue your goals. If the mind feels love or gratitude the physical aspects would be but are not limited to; calm, peace, relief, and optimistic energy, it is with that vibration that one should seek to pursue his goals with.

The point that can be taken is that it all starts from the mind. If you can somehow control the way in which you perceive something i.e. in a positive light and if subsequently you can get the heart to agree that perception or emotion then you will feel the physical effects of this. A more spiritualist view would push this point further and say that the vibration is what will be attracted to you. So a negative agreement will bring about its results and a positive agreement will attract like a magnet positive results. It is the whole idea behind you are your thoughts. So I think.

Remember there are emotions and there are physical states of beings, one should not conflate the two but rather observe them and what triggers them.

10. Bow and arrow

Think of it this way, the mind is the spotter and the heart is the sniper. Wherever the spotter tells the sniper to fire he will fire. If the spotter has been compromised, so accordingly the sniper's shot will be unreliable. All the power is found in the heart but where you direct this power will be controlled by the mind. So ask yourself what are your default thoughts. What do you think? Why do you think it? What is your train of thought?

The lens at which you look at the world. Is it a negative one or is it positive? As explained above the mind attempts to look into the foreseeable future using historical data gathered also known as your past experience and the emotions you attached to these experiences. If your past has been littered with negative experiences or you perceived it as such then all your mind has to go on are these negative (maybe traumatic) events. Similarly, if you were fortunate enough to have a predominantly positive childhood or past then you will find it easier to look at the world with a positive outlook (positive lens). As mentioned above the heart will usually follow the mind. It is through your lens or outlook that your perceptions and thoughts start to form. You then develop emotions around these thoughts and so it continues on the cycle and perpetuates further. So the lesson here is to be mindful of your thoughts and made-up maladaptive daydreamy scenarios.

You may ask well how do you train your mind to be positive if you only have negative experiences to draw from. Think of this, do not draw from the past if this is the case as the good has yet to come and your mind as it is now cannot fathom these good experiences that it has not yet experienced, therefore in this regard the mind is an unreliable source. So do not believe it when it comes to looking into your unknown future.

Time is moving through you in a similar way the pieces of the world can be thought of as moving around you rather than you navigating around it. Being mindful of your thoughts and looking solely through a positive lens and fulfilling the mind and heart agreement one now vibrates at a higher level of positivity. The intangible world meaning the story that you are living out will move around you in such a way as to match your vibration, thereby more positive outcomes and positivity in general will be attracted into your life.

How? Well in a more rational sense, one could say that you are not being emotionally reactive to a seemingly negative event but rather learning from it and looking at the positive in the bad. The idea is to train yourself to only look for and allow yourself to be emotionally reactive to the positive and simply learn from the negative without reacting emotionally thereby taking the power away from it. It sounds very obvious, but putting it into practice can be quite tedious and cumbersome at first. So, practice until the machine that is your mind does it automatically for you.

As human beings, we fail to understand what we are. So what are we? I like to think we are the observer, the host of the body and mind. So we are not the body nor the mind but rather we use it as our vehicle to navigate and traverse through the physical world. We often identify as our physical capabilities and characteristics. It makes sense, our sense of self-importance comes from how much we can affect the environment around us, and it is somewhat directly correlated to the physical capabilities and characteristics that we bear.

But when you look at the world and find what people truly want is to feel a positive emotion be it love, joy or even a quick dopamine hit. Just think about drugs. It essentially is a bottled-up form of emotion. In that way, everyone is an addict chasing or pursuing a feeling or emotion that makes us feel good. For the most part that is all there is to our lives.

How many times can you feel good? And that's it. We mask this with the story of our lives i.e passing a test at school, trying to be popular, seeking validation, making money, becoming a doctor or a lawyer. These stages of life can be denoted as us chasing a positive feeling. But to what end? It will always dissipate. You will always adapt to the feeling of good, no matter how intense, it will eventually become the norm. Akin to the addict you will seek more joy. Your joy tolerance has increased.

Everything around me is a stimulus gauging a physical, mental, or emotional response. My mind is the only thing that allows the stimulus to affect me. If it cannot penetrate my mind, it will have no power to affect me. Mastery of the mind particularly the emotions does not mean suppression but rather being able to reach an emotional state without any external stimuli be it tangible or intangible.

To a human being the external world can be thought of in two categories the first being the tangible world i.e. the trees, the ground, and the atmosphere around us etc. subsequently, the intangible world i.e the story that we make up about ourselves and the environment in our minds, our friendships and bonds etc. What's even more fascinating is the vast myriad of intense emotions that lay in the intangible facet of the external world through the story of our continuing lives. The crazy thing is the story only takes place in our heads. In that way, we can think of the outside as an illusion that is being recreated by our minds predominantly our perceptions of our stories or as the Hindus say maya.

What I see in front of me is only there because my mind processes it and creates it perfectly to be there. Should the mind be defective or different in processing capabilities and recreate something else it would be so. In theory, everyone could see something different when looking at the same object, perhaps not a great difference in shape but maybe color and texture and we would not know. Likewise, the intangible world is far more nuanced. But far more controllable. If you pass an exam, you feel happy or elated but why? why can you not feel that way without the exam? The exam is not physical, it is in your mind. In theory, if you could control your emotions, you could feel that way all of the time. Your story and how you perceive it is up to you.

11. Emotional control

Everything is within me it is just that I cannot yet tap into it as it is too far and incomprehensible. And being intangible adds to its difficulty.

As expressed above we have;

An Emotional state

And

A State of being (in a basic, rudimentary sense, feeling hot, cold are a state of being)

One may trigger the other. In theory, all we know about the triggers to emotions are those that occupy the external world. These lead to somewhat finite emotional responses i.e. fears, love, joy anger, etc, which can alter one's state of being.

What if there are more unlocked emotions within? To elaborate, what if there are far more emotional states within us that are simply inaccessible to the outside world? (remember the external world being tangible and intangible).

What if emotions are far more nuanced and intense than what we thought?

Imagine there may be different states of being that arise from these new emotions. An example would be the ineffable, state of enlightenment and much more.

Think about it what is enlightenment if you had to describe it? Maybe peace. That's all we can say about it. Perhaps it is that enlightenment cannot be triggered by the external Maya. But can only be accessed from within oneself. If so few of us ever delved within then there will not be enough information to go on about it and we will lack nomenclature or terms to explain the vast infinity that dwells within.

It is this author's opinion that emotions arising from the external world are common and felt in the same or a similar way as another individual. Whereas emotions that are triggered from the internal world (so to speak) are like fingerprints and would be felt differently by other individuals.

Gaining access to your internal control room. Not only can we entertain the possibility of new emotions being found but we may also be able to control the existing emotions that we have without the need for an external stimulus and create our own experiences. The best part is that it is all being done from within and with far greater accuracy and control. At that point, you do not need anything but sustenance and basic bodily requirements. One can now become whole in that you can choose to feel whatever you want whenever you want in whatever level of intensity you choose. Literally creating your own experiences.

The idea of monks being able to control their body temperature. When one feels intense fear or embarrassment or a combination of the two you will find that the body temperature increases i.e. public speaking may cause you to feel hot and break out into a cold sweat irrespective of the room temperature. In that way you are basically controlling your body temperature, it is just that you are involuntarily using emotions to do so as such it has far less accuracy and control. Now imagine if you could control these emotions and by extensions how you physically feel (state of being).

So how do we find the triggers or emotions from within? Meditation is one aspect. Delving within. Stripping away the ego and overcoming the primal desires that are innate in us is one way of doing so.

The spiritualists talk about the chakras and that we have 7 chakra points. As soon as a non-spiritualist person hears this he turns away. But if he listened to what it means tossing away all preconceived notions and biases and instead looked with an open mind, he may find nuggets of gold.

So, it is believed that these chakras are blocked by fear, shame, guilt, anger, desire, and trauma. To release his chakras, he must do shadow work and delve into himself naturally looking for and working through his trauma and desires. In this way, the trauma we bear and the demons we have can be used to help us work through our basic low vibrational emotions. Whatever you believe in, it will always be worthwhile to release and overcome these emotions. In doing so you will find liberation of the mind.

I think it is by releasing these emotions and unblocking your chakra points that you will be able to start gaining access to your internal control room.

There are many ways to unblock them. One is through meditation; another is through therapy but you could do so alone. Releasing is key here. You must let it go. It does not serve you. The emotions themselves are a bind or chain on your soul. Free yourself and it is by letting go that you will gain control. That is how you look at trauma as an opportunity for growth. In theory the greater the trauma the harder it will be to let go and inevitably the greater control you will end up having once you have let it go.

I appreciate that it is not that simple, it can be a hard endeavour but it is possible if you try. Most people seek to block it out i.e. through alcohol, drugs, and other distractions but it is a wasted opportunity. Do not block out trauma but sit in the discomfort and work through it. It is only by sitting in those feelings and bringing them to the surface that you can let them go.

Sometimes you must dig into yourself and your past relentlessly and ask yourself why you feel a certain way. Remember to do this as the observer of yourself i.e. without bias or excuses.

It can be a slow and gruelling process for some but for other gifted individuals letting go can be done in an instant. You won't know unless you try.

Living with it will dampen your experience on this earth. So do away with it and enjoy the very finite amount of time you have left.

0% control: quite frankly this is wearing your emotions on your sleeve. Being unable to control how it affects you.

25% control: Control through suppression. Simple suppression with no understanding.

50% control: allowing the emotions to flow through you and willingly letting them go. Not attaching to them.

75% control: being able to feel any emotion you so choose without needing an external source to do so.

100% control (Transmuting): conversion of other people's emotions i.e. fear to love. Fear is contagious. You could infect someone with fear. If they are of low emotional control this could hurt them. But if they have decent control, they could choose to let it go or redirect that fear into another emotion. If you think of emotions as energy that can neither be destroyed nor created then it can be converted into a better and more pleasant emotion. As you get better at understanding your own emotions, you will find more nuance in it i.e. the vast array of positive emotions that exist other than happiness such as; Contentment, Interest, Amusement, and Serenity. You may then decide to redirect these negative emotions that you are assimilating from others into positive ones.

I am not saying to go out of your way to drain people of their emotional energy but rather it can be used to protect you and your mental state from psychological harm. Furthermore, with this level of control, you will naturally be able to block out the emotions of others and choose whether or not to accept them.

12. Enlightenment

When others see an enlightened being or one who is close to enlightenment their soul recognises them and seeks to follow or reject that being. The soul or the observer within you is drawn to the enlightened one, they gravitate towards him so that they may also find liberation. We yearn to learn from them and to be free, for the enlightened ones are rare to come by. Those that we know as having reached enlightenment have lived through our stories across the globe as gods. Shri Krishna, Jesus, The original Siddharth Gautama Buddha, and all his derivatives.

What does it mean to be enlightened? You see this term is ineffable. Only very few of us have reached this state of being and have shared the experience. In my opinion, it may be a very high level of peace, serenity and contentment simply in being. Not in being alive but simply in existing at that very moment. The idea is not to desire anything or fear anything. This may leave one perplexed as to what one should do with their time. For that, I would suggest following the highest passion but that too is a desire. The Buddhists would say to sleep when you are tired, eat when you are hungry, and move your bowels when you feel the need to.

It is my opinion that when one reaches enlightenment, he unlocks his internal world. Upon doing so his time is spent in meditation wandering and exploring the realms that lie within him thereby all he has to do is maintain his physical body.

When enlightenment is present it takes over the whole being; the mind, body, and soul. Thereby there is no room for any other emotion.

You will no longer feel nor embody fear and the same will apply to happiness. That is one of the things that scare those who titter on the border to enlightenment is that when they leap there is no going back to feeling the other low vibrational emotions.

If you feel happy you must also be ready to bear the feeling of sadness. But enlightenment is a baseline emotion. There is no other side to it. It is complete and whole on its own. It makes you realise your wholeness and, in that way, you need nothing from the world and you realise you were everything all along. You gain control by giving it up as letting go of control is one of the steps towards enlightenment. Your desire and ego will be absolved. You will develop a new perception.

13. Live die repeat

The live die and repeat theory. If one were to live, die, and be reborn to the same life with the exact same factors and bearing the memory of his previous life he would do things better no doubt. But better how? My take is that most people would act to fuel the ego's needs. They would take advantage of the memory of their previous attempt at the same life and move to make far more money and develop their education and skill set that they would have found lacking in the previous life and find more suitors in sexual escapades and enjoy more cozy, luxurious life. Say they die and are reborn again to the same conditions (with memory intact), they would repair mistakes they had made in the previous repeat and fuel more public recognition, validation approval, undergo all the life hacks they have discovered, and more things to the ego's content. He does whatever he can to nourish the body and mind leaving the soul to starve

Eventually, with enough repeats, he gets bored of the same things as the things that satisfy the ego are finite. He has exhausted every facet and external stimuli be it women, money, drugs, alcohol and validation, etc that is available to him. This would also hold true should the person occupy different bodies encompassing different stories at different times with the same repeated memories. It would simply take more time for the ego to be exhausted.

Stage Two. Eventually, the occupier of the body would no longer have any care for what satiates the ego, he no longer cares as he has seen it all, and understands how frivolous and empty he feels at the end of it. He may simply wish for death but continues to be reborn.

Having no success with rebirths he now looks to and values relationships and connections over everything else as he finds profound meaning to this. He notices and associates with everyone enjoys the company of those whom he may have disregarded in his past lives and draws empathy for those who adhere to the egotistical nature he once shared. He finds that he is a better judge of character and that those around him have more substance and integrity to them as opposed to the vultures and vain individuals he once associated with.

However, no matter the shift in his mindset he is still not free from the accursed rebirth. So, he continues on his nomadic quest finding and building new relationships everywhere simply to understand that even this has an end to it. Even human relationships are finite.

The third stage. Having exhausted every external stimulus that the world can produce for him he continues to wonder with despair in his heart he stops and decides finally to ponder within through what we know as meditation. He journeys within himself and finds that there are new internal stimuli, emotions, and states of being that cannot be ascertained from the outside. This time it is different. What he finds within is infinite. There is no end to it, he is finally connected to himself and detached from everything outside. He no longer desires for anything. Not to live, not to die, not for relationships, and certainly not for anything the ego wants. Now what? He does not care as he has reached peace or enlightenment. This time as he closes his eyes he leaves for good. He has found liberation. Well done to him!

Now imagine if he did not have any recollection of his past lives, how hard would it be then? How would he know? It doesn't matter. See the purpose of this book is to help you liberate your mind. Try to learn from this story so you may tap into the infinite that lies within.

14. Everyone is me

Have you ever heard the saying or the theory that everyone is you? I never really understood or got it. I just thought of it as a form or concept of oneness. But as I grew older and realised that everything begins and ends in the mind. Then it is very possible that everyone is just a projection of your mind or a reflection of your inner world.

You see as will be explained further, everything thing is created twice firstly in reality and then in the mind. That is from the point of view of the spectator, not the originator. Most of us are the spectators. So, the person we see in front of us is subject to our biases and experiences and the genetic factors that influence the mind. We cannot see the person in front of us for what they are. In addition, this person may be capped by their expression of self and may not be able to show the world just yet their most authentic self. This could be due to several reasons i.e. acting from ego, trauma, fear, confidence issues and not being able to communicate effectively among other things. On both ends, we cannot truly see each other. We are hiding in plain sight.

In an old Buddhist story, a man leaves his village. He takes route to another neighbouring village. Before entering he sees an old man outside. He asks the old man "What kind of people reside in this village"? The old man replies "Well what kind of people resided in your previous village"? he said, "egotistical and corrupt people were in my old village". The Old man said "Well there are the same people in this village". Another man came to this village and asked the old man the same question. The old man responded in the same way. This time however the stranger said

"Good and loving people resided in my old village" The old man said, "well the same kinds of people are in this one".

How could this be? Well, the old man understood that both men had different lenses and perspectives on life and that they simply saw a reflection of themselves and so they could not perceive anything more than what was already within. You may ask that objectively both men could be right about the people of their village. But in this example, they painted every individual with the same brush and not just one in particular.

Now ask yourself how are the people in your city, village, or even your household. Ask yourself how you view the world. And you will find out how you view yourself.

Now that is not to say if someone punches you in the face that is your inner world doing that. It's not. Lol.

15. Simulation

There is an idea floating around that we are in a simulation, this is commonly known as simulation theory. This is the notion that we are in a computer program being controlled by an entity outside our comprehension.

What does a computer program mean? Does it have to mean electronics and gadgets and screens and motherboards and all things associated with tech? well no. It could be a computer program adjacent system for lack of a better term. At least that is my take on the matter.

Another term floating around is the "matrix". The matrix is not to be confused with the simulation but rather it is part of the simulation. The matrix in our common and misaligned understanding is said to be the materialistic allures that life provides from sex, to the money to cars to fame, glory, and validation. This is a misconception. In fact, by seeking and worshiping only these things we fall prey to the system that is the matrix. you see the matrix is in the mind and not outside. It is you v you. There is no one else around. That is the trick of the game.

The Sanskrit word for the matrix is "Maya" meaning the illusion. It all begins and ends in the mind. The mind is the author of your fortune and misfortune, it is you the holder and occupier of your mind that decides what will be written in your story.

It is not that you should have disdain for the allures of the Maya but rather not to worship or marvel init.

The matrix is the ego and all things that inflate it. Do not get lost. Understand to look within and break free from it.

"Had I done it differently it would be out of fear that no one would understand. I tend to regret actions done out of fear." This quote came from a man who responded in this way when confronted with the fear of missing out (FOMO). This fear is usually the perpetrator of a lot of our anxiety and misdoings. Remember this quote when you try to do something because of FOMO.

Infe/supe complex. No one is superior or inferior we just happen to be. Perhaps we do things with different skillsets and to a different degree of competence but that does not make some more or less significant than others. In this author's unlicensed opinion, one may think of the superiority and inferiority complex as synonymous in that it takes the same mindset to reach either one. I.e a person who has a superiority complex can very easily shift to the inferior one if their metric of valuation for determining their complex is broken. I.e you are the best at basketball in your league and you develop this sense of superiority because of it but due to an outside occurrence, there happens to be other players that enter your league who are far better. You now develop insecurities around this complex which can soon and very easily shift to an inferiority complex, unless you are delusional in thinking you are the best. Neither is healthy. In the West, It is seen as a good thing to have a superiority complex in business or sports but as explained it may not end well.

You, reading this! You may not think you have a complex. You may not for all I know. Heres my test. I want you to ask yourself do you believe deep inside that you are better than a homeless drug addict who lives under a bridge? Most people may not admit it outright but deep down they may believe so. But why? Is it because you have a home, more money, dress better have more public recognition etc? Find out why. When you do you will understand the metric at which you derive self-valuation. You will find that there exist others who are more accomplished in the categories that you self-evaluate thus the insecurities and inferiority complex start to take form. Does that mean they are better than you? No.

So, ask yourself again are you inferior or superior to the homeless crackhead? No. You just possess different things, and have access to a different array of options. You may even develop an understanding and empathy for him in that he is just a guy who took a different path than you for whatever reason. When you are able to throw your metric for valuation out the window you will no longer feel inferior or superior but rather develop a more profound understanding and empathy for people in a different position than you. You are thereby liberated from your own judgment.

That is important, liberating you from the judgment and opinions of others but far more importantly freeing yourself from your own judgment and opinions both consciously and subconsciously.

If you have developed empathy or have it by nature. Well done! Empathy is one of the greatest superpowers a human being can possess. You can put yourself in the shoes of another and experience what they would have, thereby growing as a result. You can use someone else's experience to feel how they would have felt, navigate through the complexity of emotions they would have, and gather and learn the lessons of their experience without having to go through it yourself. But it is a double-edged blade if you do not have a good grip and understanding of your mind, emotions, and mindset (complex/insecurities) then these foreign experiences will do more harm than good i.e. causing you second-hand trauma and exacerbating whatever fears and insecurities you may have. So ensure you do your shadow work before you activate the superpower of empathy.

The human mind is capable of great things it is just that from the day we are born, limitations after limitations are placed on us. Think about it our mental understanding and comprehension of concepts are limited namely through the language that we speak. We speak to express ourselves and our thoughts. But we learn through the expression itself. What does that mean? It means that we are learning to express the thought as the confines of the method of expression allow us to, and not to first learn the entirety of the concept before understanding how to express it.

As such we have limited the learning process to begin with. As far as I know, there are no other ways of learning but through the limited expression, we have created. Think about how much is left in the void.

A more overt way of thinking about this would be to take a look at a study done on a tribe in Africa. Their language did not contain a word for the color blue. They were shown 6 squares 5 were green and 1 was blue. They could not differentiate between the blue and the green squares. Now you could say that they simply thought of blue as another shade of green and most likely they could not see the difference in colour as they were limited by the language that they spoke.

That study is troubling, think about it practically, how much colour are we blind to? Go even further how much of a concept do we not see simply because we cannot differentiate between the blue and the green so to speak?

What other limitations are there?

Ego

Preconceived notions

Bias

16. Embody what you want to see in others and attract that reaction.

Your perception of the world is a projection of your thoughts. What you see and observe in others more often than not is a projection of what you see in yourself. For example, if you notice a dislikable trait in someone that trait is within you otherwise you would not have the ability to identify it. That trait may be buried within yourself hidden from you or you have found and overcome it so now you can see it in others.

Likewise, a positive trait that you have observed in another that you wished you had, is already within yourself, you simply have to uncover and develop it. When you see a confident individual how do you know that they are confident? Is it the way they walk, talk, and other micro-movements and behavioral patterns that you pick up on? You can only pick up on them because they are also within you.

If you cannot imagine yourself doing something, it is likely, you do not believe that you are capable of it. Now you must change your perception and current belief system about yourself so you can imagine being the person who is capable of doing the things you want. If you can not imagine landing a job or being in a relationship with someone, then you need to understand why it is you think this way and work on your skills, physique, beliefs, and thought patterns to become the person in your mind that is capable of getting your desire.

Even if you do get the job or relationship you wanted if you still have the current belief system about yourself, it will do you no good as you will develop insecurities and fear around it. You will not be able to be present and truly enjoy the position you are in instead you will be constantly bombarded with the fear of not being good enough and anxiety will develop about losing what you have.

Further into this you may end up feeling undeserving and imposter syndrome will start to creep up on you. So you must redress the issues at hand that make you think you are not worthy. This process is laid out like this;

Change your beliefs about yourself. Do this by shifting your perception. Shift your perception by looking at the why and how you think the way you do about yourself. From there start doing the work that will change or remove the "why" and "how" as these are what confirm your beliefs about yourself.

It does take work depending on the individual and their past experiences.

But just remember that most of us are insecure about something.

So like Bob Marley sang "Don't worry, about a thing, cause every little thing is gonna be alright".

Take it easy. Relax and breathe.

You're doing just fine.

17. A smile attracts a smile

How you want others to react to you is how you should react to others. Smile if you want to be smiled at, be jovial if you want to attract jovial people.

You must embody the trait or emotion you want to receive. Remember to truly embody an emotion your heart and mind must be aligned.

Embody and demonstrate the emotions and behaviour you want to be reflected on you.

That is why controlling your emotions to at least 75% control is necessary to allow you to feel the way you want most of the time.

18. What does the soul remember

When you die You take the process with you, not the results. The lessons learned and bonds forged along the way will be engraved in your soul but the result being materialistic in nature, they stay here. You see the bonds and lessons they serve to unlock the mystery within yourself particularly the vast information and emotions that otherwise you would not have access to. For example, most of us know not of unconditional and selfless love until we have children of our own. You could say that it is the bonds we forged with our kids that allow us to unlock this feeling or vibration. That feeling is etched into our souls and we carry that on with us.

19. Debates over religion

God creates man, man creates religion and religion bears fruit to segregation not just amongst other religious groups but within one's religion itself. Why? Because man has an adversarial nature to resolve everything, be it religious debates, politics, or legal matters.

Religious debates in particular are a total fallacy in my opinion. What exactly is one arguing? Is it that their god is real? Or is it that their god and religion is the true way? Or is it that their stories are more likely to have happened than the other guy's stories? You see these defeats the purpose of spirituality or religion if you conflate them.

The idea that you can prove the existence of God is disrespectful to God himself whatever your religious belief may be. God is an ineffable and incomprehensible, intangible and formless being so far as all our religions can agree. The idea of belief and faith is that it is blind. You believe and have faith despite not knowing with proof or evidence. You believe despite there being no hard facts on that matter. You are not supposed to know, that is by design, so I think. You are only supposed to believe through faith alone. You can't make anyone believe through faith, if they find God or faith whatever that means to them, they will have to do so of their own volition.

Faith or belief cannot exist if you know. If you know or can prove something to be then you remove faith out of the equation.

It is not my job to convince you or anyone else that God exists and that he does in the way I perceive. Even if I wanted to, I could not see as I stand now, as a human being. I do not possess the faculties, the nuanced forms of expression that are beyond our languages, and much more. So,

I simply believe and I am grateful that where it is I reside allows me the freedom of expression to practice my religious beliefs.

20. The misconception of the Hindu faith

The divine. God. The intangible, formless, and ineffable being. The different forms of god are manifested into physical beings to assist humankind in a way they can look to comprehend. How can one understand or worship a concept? I.e the Hindus worship the stone known as the Shiva Linga. Most misunderstand it. What it is, is the concept of creation that they look at as a form of shiva. Through the worship of this idol, we can try to understand the concept of creation and thereby one of the faces or angles of the supreme god known as Brahman. This is the ultimate infinite, it is formless, genderless, and intangible. This is the monotheistic nature of Hinduism. The Hindus do not believe that the idols themselves are gods. The idols are a place where we can accumulate and target our faith. A place where we can worship the supreme infinite formless god Brahman.

All of the Hindu gods are concepts and are a different face or manifestation of the one supreme being. That is the idea that all is one. They simply have one God that they worship in many ways. The mother's instinct, the concept of creation, the different stages of womanhood (Nirvartri), father time. How can we humans worship or come to know these faces of God or begin to understand the nuances in them, so we are aided through the idols and through the stories we are told? So the manifestation of the different forms of god to be assigned to these concepts gives us a better understanding of the other aspects of Brahman.

These symbols or statues or idols whatever you want to call them are aids to help us get closer to God, to remember the concepts that the idols represent, and they help us pass down these stories and concepts to our descendants. In addition, the idols as symbols do not get lost in translation as words do. They help to bridge the gap between humanity and the infinite.

We see God in everything the wind, the ground the air the sun, Mother Nature and even death.

You see I think that all religions eventually come to the same end in that we reach and intended target, the same god, it is just that our methods of worship are different.

As humans, we like to categorize things, put them into boxes, and label them. That is how we have religions i.e. Hinduism, Islam, Protestants, Catholics, etc. Without confining yourself to a religion say for a moment that you are spiritual. What you are saying by my understanding is that you are subscribing to the theory of oneness and that god operates outside the realm of religion.

Religion is man-made. Man attempts to characterize and capture God. God is an infinite concept that goes beyond the grey matter of your mind. He cannot be captured by man. However man is stubborn, he fears death and longs for community due to his instincts to survive. This causes him to find meaning and refuge not in god but in religion. If you seek god then overcome your primal instincts. Religion attaches to the ego and God dwells where the ego is absent.

All religions lead to the same road and there are many methods of worship that one can choose to undertake but what is truly important is to live a life of virtue.

One can worship his God by watering a plant or by exercising. You see God is in everything. By exercising and choosing to prolong the longevity of your life you a creation of God honour and love yourself and in doing so also honour God. Feeding a homeless man or playing with your pet, all of which could be a way in which you choose to worship.

Your relationship with God is particular to you and different to your brothers. You could live under the same roof and practice the same religion as your brother but still, your relationship to God will be different whether slightly or greatly. This is due to your differing perceptions altogether. God will mean something different to you. In this world, there are 8 billion perceptions of God all particular to each individual.

Now this is what I believe. Not all Hindus believe the same way. Just this author's take.

21. The adversarial nature of man

O ne side fights the other and the better debater wins. A debate by nature demands for there to be a winner and loser mostly determined by the people watching the debate. But people are vain and usually lack the ability to critically analyse a topic with true objectivity as such they tend to fall victim to the most likable individual.

Sitting on the fence. I think the fence is the best place to be. On the fence, you will have a better view of either side and be able to denote the pros and cons of everything and thus come to a more balanced objective point of view. But our longing for community, bias, and the influence of people leads us to pick a side, we are ostracised if we do not choose a side. We are labeled as indecisive and from a business point of view our revenue could be impacted, so we fall into the game of this side vs that side.

Prove me wrong: the sky is green

I believe this is a good debating tool. To win you have to stretch facts and come up with creative and colourful arguments to prove your outlandish points. It also makes the debate fun and prevents you from being too emotionally invested in it. Now if you ever have a debate with someone, you are well equipped with a mind that has trained and been cultivated to approach debates in a creative, fun, and imaginative way.

The problem with this is that it trains the mind to be right and not to be factually correct. It means that you will debate for the sole purpose of being right and winning and not to look to be fair and show an accurate representation of the topic or issue. This means you will be a good debater but not a good problem solver. Sure you can make your bullshit make sense and that is a good skill to possess but you may lose yourself in it and inevitably lose the ability to effectively problem solve.

22. Van Gogh dreams the painting and then paints the dream. "Everything is created twice"

Everything is created twice once in reality and once in your mind. But do we ever see the stand-alone piece that sits in reality? Most probably not. Do we have the ability to be objective? I don't think so. I think it is beyond the capabilities of a human being. Think of a painting. There lies the painting in reality then there lies the painting in the perception of our minds. We only have true access to the painting through the lens of perception that resides in our minds. We cannot see the painting that sits in reality.

Such is the curse and blessing that befalls us. Everything including ourselves is at the mercy of our perceptions. Everyone will perceive the painting in their own way and thus we see differently what sits in one way. The more talented of us have the gift of empathy therefore we can to some degree be open enough to perceive the painting in many other ways not just through the dogmatic singular lens.

Now think of how complex a human being is in comparison to a painting. The levels and layers of bias, life experience, culture, language, genetic composition, vulnerabilities, etc, that make us who we are. In that way we can never truly know another individual. What you see in them and what I see in them are two different things.

A human perception within reason is an unreliable thing so be careful not to depend too heavily on it. That is not to say ignore your instincts or intuition but rather try to broaden your perception and develop an open mind to negate the negative effects of a harsh perception.

How I think that the quote from Van Gogh was supposed to be taken was that he will dream the painting and try to the best of his capabilities to capture the entirety of the dream on his canvas. You see the dream will then be watered down and parts of it lost due to the limited capabilities of the artist and the limitations of the 3-dimensional plane that we call reality. In addition, say that he could capture the dream in all its dimensions, would the spectator or audience be able to perceive it as intended by the artist? Probably not, due to his unique perception as explained above.

However, with the gift or talent of empathy, he will be able to discern what the artist was going for and see things through his eyes. An amazing trait to have.

Perhaps things are created three times. Once in the mind of the originator, once in reality, and once in the minds of those beholding the painting.

It begs the question, where does the dream come from? What sparks the creative artful thought? From a spiritualist point of view, it is the soul trying to relay knowledge through intention. It is said that in a sleep state, a human being relinquishes their ego and control simultaneously putting them in a state of trust in the universe. Thereby they are in a state where the soul or higher self can relay knowledge to them through their mind without having to undergo the harsh perception that is derived from their ego.

23. Live your life to your highest passion but adhere within the confines of duty in that way you find balance.

L ive your life searching for your passions and seek to take it to the very edge that it can take you. Most people get lost in the story that was set for them by circumstance and lose connection to their innermost authentic selves. Some call this version of self to be your inner child or your higher self. You must seek him out. It will guide you to the most enjoyable path that you can't even fathom. How? Simply by trying your inner self will be aware or awaken to your call. But endeavor to believe that it is there for this to work.

You see your most authentic self is covered right now by many veils be it trauma, fear, ego, desire, malintent, anger, grudges, or seeking frivolous and vain things like public validation. You must work with yourself or remove these veils. You will find that as you work through these issues it will be easier to identify your passions and pursue them.

The Buddhists have a saying that spirituality or meditation is not for gain but to remove these things from the body and mind and in essence free the soul.

24. You want to be like the wise

Wisdom brings about peace and intellect brings about suffering.

What is the difference between the two? Intellect is the gathering and application of information around us. Wisdom is the understanding and application of the knowledge that lies within us. With wisdom comes open-mindedness, shifts in perception, control of mindset, and among other things mastery of one's mind.

With intellect comes the exploration of the external, seeing the external as the source and material of all. With the infinite nature of the universe and knowledge as a whole and the inability to separate oneself from his ego, the man who simply dwells in intellect will be subject to the sways of the tides of other men. He will be bogged down by preconceived notions, and assumptions and lose the ability to adopt different perspectives. In his quest to satiate his hunger to find meaning outside of himself, he will be lost.

The wise one will find the answer within himself, with the understanding that all begins and ends in his mind. He will be closer to peace. That is not to say look only within. Sure, it is a great start and end. However, the universe requires balance in all things. So, as you dwell within also display focus outside. Do not be dogmatic in your approach to simply follow the rules in fear of shame and ridicule.

One could say wisdom is another form of intellect, but I like it this way.

25. Seeing God

Most religions denote the enemy or evil in the form of a snake. I do not think it is a literal snake. I think entering the mouth of the snake and being swallowed whole by it means you have become one with your ego. You are now ruled and controlled by your ego. Your actions will come from selfishness.

I believe that there are two snakes. The other leads you into the mouth of the first and guides you further and further along the body of the snake. It does this in two ways it will stroke your ego with the materialistic allures and validation of the world. The second way is that it invokes fear that originates from your desires.

The first snake can be beaten by separating yourself from your ego. In doing this you will be spat out by the snake. Maybe you are not fully merged with your ego but you still overlap with it and are not completely separate yet. So, think to separate yourself from it. Ask yourself how?

Usually, we do not beat the second snake, but rather we learn to tame it. Taming the fears and desires. But if you want to beat Snake Two then surrender your desires. Practice detachment and detach from your desires. Upon doing this you will find yourself to have become a new person with a completely changed persona. People in general may not understand you and where you are coming from. Remove desire and destroy fear. Fear can only play off of your desires. Desires lead you to succumb to your ego.

Looking at things with the ego means that you are only looking at things superficially and only seeing what these things or people can do for you.

Depending on how far merged you are with the ego you may find it difficult to separate. The ego does not want you to know that it is the problem. It will try to delude you into thinking that you are the greatest or it will make you believe that you are irreparable. Do not believe it either way. Think of the ego as the venom suit from Spider-Man. Venom is this parasite that attaches to your skin and does not want to detach. At first, it feels good to have your ego stroked but then it changes who you are originally. You cannot be your true self with the suit on. The venom suit will attack everything that threatens to remove it from its host. At a certain point, the suit will take over and your actions will purely be from ego/selfish desire.

Masters have not only detached from the suit but destroyed the parasite through permanent ego death. And that is usually the answer to it. But separating yourself from the ego and keeping it alive will let you use the ego to your advantage. Say you gain full control and exert your will over the venom suit, now you have a tremendous advantage. You can utilize all the emotions of the ego in whatever way you choose. But more importantly, you gain the power of discernment. This power increases your intuition and allows you to discern the actions and intentions of those around you who are led by their ego.

To separate you must become the observer. In doing this you will naturally be able to kill the ego whenever you choose. You see at this point you take true ownership of your mind in doing this you can roam around it freely.

From a spiritualist standpoint, there is a reason for everything. There is a reason that we have the ego. We must learn to overcome it. When we use the tools of the body and mind to overcome the obstacle of the ego, this progress is relayed to the soul and now it will learn to see clearer. If you can see things for what they are, the illusion for the illusions, the allures for the allures, the snake for the snake then you are one step closer to being able to see God. Looking at the substance of things and not predetermining value from the surface or what it can do for you. This will put you in a state of gratitude.

26. I surrender

This state of being is called surrendering. By surrendering in every way, you gain control over the ego and can make it work for you. It is one of the solutions to this puzzle. Surrendering control will give you control.

The ego serves as a barrier, not between you and other people but between you and yourself. It prevents you from true spiritual growth. The ego death is one way to remove this barrier. But remember the ego death is still a death meaning that it is permanent. There is no going back from this.

Surrendering is not the same as giving up. Surrendering takes courage. Surrendering occurs when you still have strength left. Your surrender is voluntary. Embody the state of surrendering. This is the closest state to enlightenment that one can achieve without killing the ego.

27. Emotional pillars

Using people to help us transmute emotional energy. I.E. No matter how angry or upset I feel when I look at my kids I feel unconditional love. You have transmuted your emotions using your relationships to help you.

I do not need anyone to make me feel loved. You see we want to be loved by others but why? It confirms in our minds that we are worthy of love and so it becomes easier to love ourselves. But remember everything begins and ends in the mind. We do not need to be tricked into loving ourselves. We can feel all the love we want by giving it to ourselves. Simply allow yourself to feel unconditional love. You see the only love you are capable of giving yourself is unconditional. Most of us do not know this feeling. It means to love without reason. It's a love that can only come from selflessness and originates outside of the ego. When you cannot give this to yourself then you are at the mercy of others to constantly confirm that you are lovable. What you are doing is giving other people power over your inner world or mind. Do not allow this.

That is not to say to refrain from loving anyone or allowing yourself to feel loved by them. If you ever do love someone, do so unconditionally. Easier said than done. But this means that you love them without expectation. Their behaviour and words have no impact on your unconditional love. Love coming from the ego, although powerful will lead to pain and suffering and potential trauma.

RESISTANCE

What is resistance? In terms of manifestation, it is considered to be the emotions or feelings you have that resist your desire. Now an example of this is imagining that your desires are a root that can grow into a tree and that as the tree grows a vine also wraps around the tree. In this example the vine is fear. The desire usually comes with fear.

So what do you do? How do you detach fear from desire? One way would be to let go of desire as a whole. But that seems too drastic a measure. There has to be a way of removing the resistance in the form of fear while maintaining the integrity and intensity of the desire.

You do this by letting go of what it is you want and how you want it to come in. You allow yourself to give life the room it needs to bring it in for you.

In addition, do not attach meaning to the desire. Remove meaning from it. For example, do not attach self-respect, self-worth, feelings of happiness, and other things of that nature to the desire. Keep the desire vague in what it means to you and specific in what it is you want.

It works both ways whether you believe in manifestation or not. From the point of view of manifestation, you are drastically lowering the resistance to the desire this way. Furthermore, from an objective, rational point of view, when your desires come to fruition you do not fear or feel anxious about what it is you have. Fear around the desire that you already possess may take the form of imposter syndrome (as mentioned before). you may end up being a self-saboteur. So, lowering your resistance helps you in all ways.

It seems like the words do not possess the power the words are just sounds. You attach meaning to the words and that meaning is what possesses power. So meaning is power. If I can control meaning i.e. giving meaning to my breath, I can create new feelings.

A word particularly an adjective has a cloud of thought or meaning behind it. For example, I am confident. It means the way I speak, walk, sound, look, dress and much more gives off the impression of confidence. I confine and attach all of this meaning into one word which is "confidence".

In terms of affirmations saying things like "I am confident", "I am strong" etc, I am supposed to help embody these traits. I think it is like punching a brick wall with your fists and hoping that at some point you will get through. Additionally, maybe by saying these affirmations you may be saying to yourself indirectly that you do not embody these things. So, it might be counterproductive.

Taking power away from words means you can relocate power to something else. You see it is meaning the cultivate emotions, not words. Maybe our thoughts are in meaning. We have thoughts that are clouds of meaning and we then use words to explain them through. Relocate and assign meaning to a particular breath. Let's say 3 inhales and one exhale mean peace to you, and so breathing in this way will mean that you can activate a certain feeling in this case peace. You can play around with this.

A belief about yourself is surrounded and created by a web of thoughts that confirm and reaffirm it to be true or likely to be true. For example, he jogged in the park in front of people, or he did this knowingly weird-looking workout at the gym today, and he spoke to this attractive girl even though he was nervous. All these actions indicate to your mind to say that you are confident and bold. It shows to yourself that you do not care about humiliating yourself in public and that you can act despite fear of rejection. With more of these actions, you will build a belief system that you are these things.

Now the actions will be different as per what the characteristics you want to embody mean to you. When you build multiple belief systems about yourself you can cause a huge perception shift. This shift will mean that you have become an entirely different person from who you once were.

The truly talented amongst us can choose to believe and disbelieve anything they want on command just like flipping a switch. That is the level of mastery they hold over their mind. They can thus change and adopt multiple perceptions that they feel the need to, this is a whole new level of empathy that most of us are not familiar with.

REACHING A POINT OF neutrality. Reaching neutrality means you will be unmoved by the external things going on around you if you so choose. In my opinion, there are two versions of neutrality one stemming from enlightenment and detachment, The other stemming from nihilism and disconnection. Despite it being neutral the former can be thought of as a positive neutrality and the latter can be thought of as a negative neutrality. They are both unmoved but one has found peace in their temporary existence on this planet, which has given them a sense of appreciation and a profound outlook on life. On the other hand, the other has found peace in the idea that nothing has meaning and nothing matters, this gives them a sense of carelessness and complacency in regards to life, in particular to the lives of others around them, hence disconnection. Nevertheless, their sense of disregard gives them nothing to attach to, thereby they have achieved neutrality. Needless to say, look for and try to attain the positive form as this will enable you to appreciate and connect to the things around you.

Along with knowledge and wisdom comes the temptation to teach or preach what you know. Resist and control this impulse. Just because you feel you know does not mean that it should be received and divulged. If you know it's because you understand and there is no way around it.

Spirituality is an individual's game. The search for God is within. You cannot go within with anyone else. You may seek spiritual teachers to help on your quest to delve within yourself. But ultimately the spiritual journey is an individual's game. You do not find God with a buddy, you do it on your own. But it's meant to be fun. So, enjoy yourself on this journey.

Think of life as a video game. The game becomes hard and stressful when you think you are the character in the game. When you take a step back and dissociate from the game you are and only then can you truly take your time and enjoy the experience. That is how I think one should lead their life. Take a step back from your situation, do not be so emotionally invested, and breathe, now progress. Take on every challenge like this and enjoy the obstacle it is there to help you grow.

Going on with the video game theory, think of the controller as the mind and the person holding the controller as you. Thereby, you are the holder of the mind. I think, we are so versatile that we can operate as the thought and the observer of that thought simultaneously.

Do not forget you are the holder of the mind.

28. See Ya

To you,

The one who has finished this book either partly or in its entirety, I wish you the best of luck going forward. I sincerely hope you have found this guide helpful in whichever way you need. Remember there is no set way of approaching the intricacies of the mind, just find a way that works for you.

Live your life to the highest passion within the confines of duty.

Just let go.

Yours Sincerely,

Darren Yoganaden Murugan

www.ingramcontent.com/pod-product-compliance
Lightning Source LLC
Chambersburg PA
CBHW031003090426
42737CB00008B/657